IN MY OWN LITTLE CORNER

Lyrics by OSCAR HAMMERSTEIN II   Music by RICHARD RODGERS

I'm as mild and as meek as a mouse, When I hear a com-mand I o-bey, But I know of a spot in my house Where no one can stand in my way.

(continued on page 30)

IN MY OWN LITTLE CORNER

RODGERS AND HAMMERSTEIN'S
IN MY OWN LITTLE CORNER

LYRICS BY
OSCAR HAMMERSTEIN II

MUSIC BY
RICHARD RODGERS

ILLUSTRATED BY
KATHERINE POTTER

SIMON & SCHUSTER BOOKS FOR YOUNG READERS

SIMON & SCHUSTER BOOKS FOR YOUNG READERS
An imprint of Simon & Schuster Children's Publishing Division
1230 Avenue of the Americas, New York, New York 10020
Text copyright © 1957 by Richard Rodgers and Oscar Hammerstein II.
Copyright renewed. International Copyright secured. Williamson Music
owner of publication and allied rights throughout the world.
Used with permission.
Illustrations copyright © 1995 by Katherine Potter.
All rights reserved including the right of reproduction
in whole or in part in any form.
SIMON & SCHUSTER BOOKS FOR YOUNG READERS
is a trademark of Simon & Schuster.
The text for this book is set in 16-point Cochin.
The illustrations were done in pastel.
Manufactured in the United States of America.

10 9 8 7 6 5 4 3 2 1

Hammerstein, Oscar, 1895–1960. [In my own little corner]
Rodgers and Hammerstein's in my own little corner / lyrics by
Oscar Hammerstein II ; music by Richard Rodgers ;
illustrations by Katherine Potter.   p. cm. Summary: While sitting in a
corner, a little girl imagines that she is a Norwegian princess, a prima
donna in Milan, a dancing mermaid, and more. 1. Children's songs—
Texts. [1. Imagination—Songs and music. 2. Songs.] I. Rodgers,
Richard, 1902– . II. Potter, Katherine, ill. III. Title PZ8.3.H1865Rn
1995 [E]—dc20 94-7633 CIP AC
ISBN: 0-671-79458-2

For Julia and Rachel:
Go to your room.

—K. P.

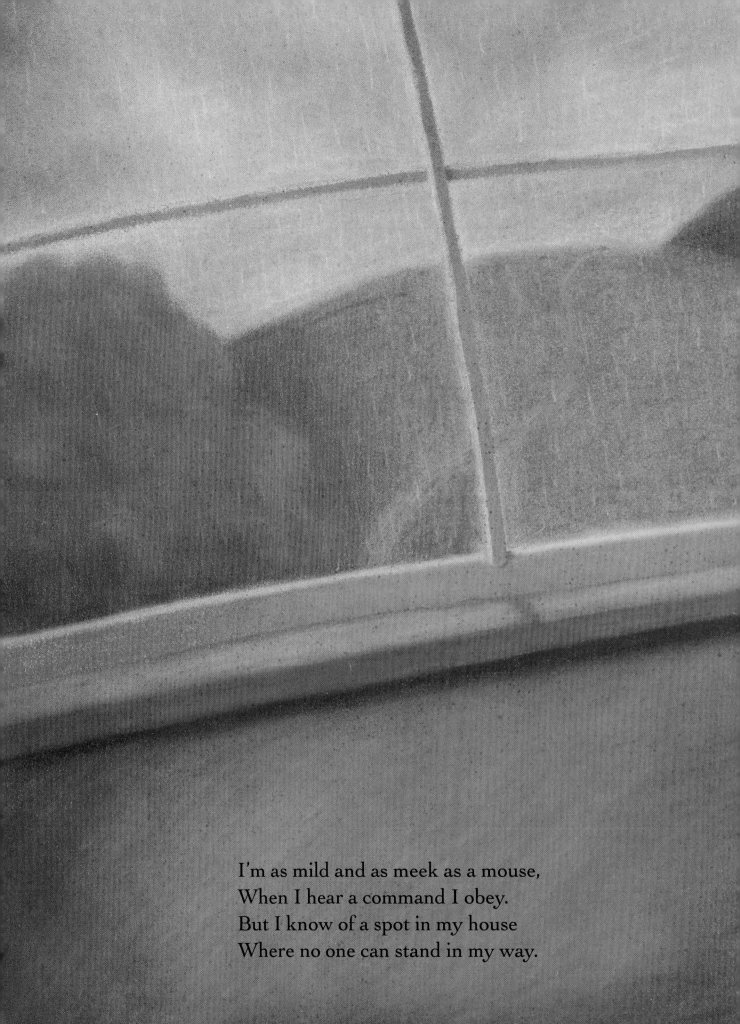

I'm as mild and as meek as a mouse,
When I hear a command I obey.
But I know of a spot in my house
Where no one can stand in my way.

In my own little corner,
In my own little chair,
I can be whatever I want to be.
On the wing of my fancy
I can fly anywhere
And the world will open its arms to me.

I'm a young Norwegian princess . . .

. . . or a milk maid,

I'm the greatest prima donna in Milan,

I'm an heiress who has always had her silk made
By her own flock of silkworms in Japan!

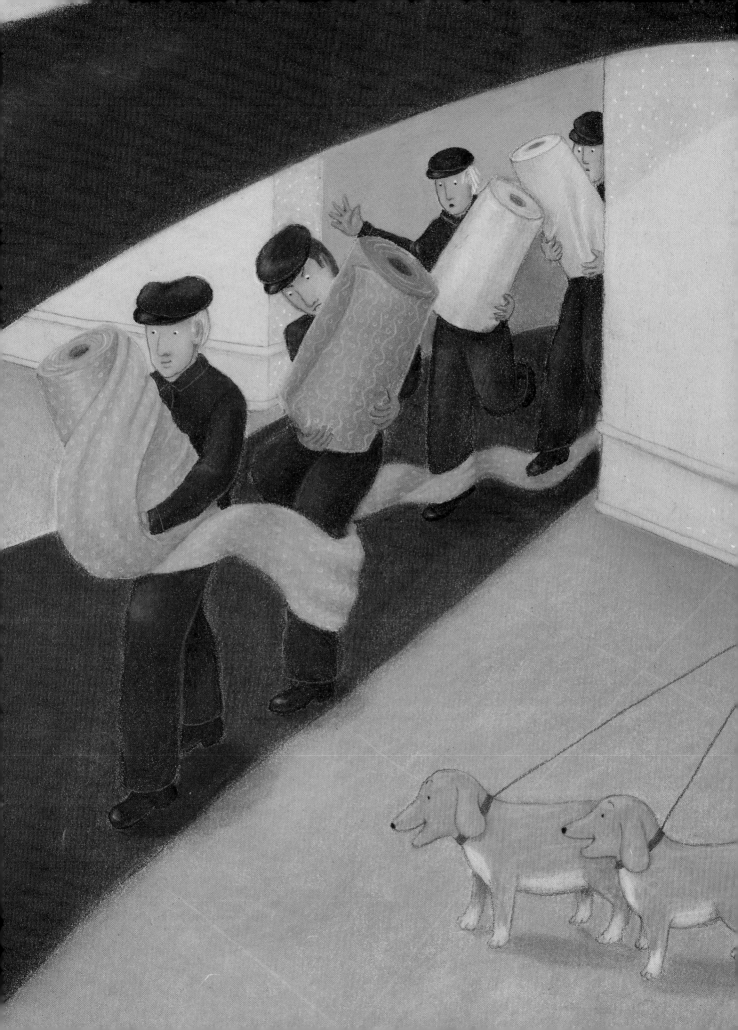

I'm a girl men go mad for,
Love's a game I can play
With a cool and confident kind of air,
Just as long as I stay
In my own little corner,
All alone
        In my own
                Little chair.

I'm a slave in Calcutta,

I'm a queen in Peru,

I'm a mermaid dancing upon the sea.

I'm a huntress on an African safari —
(It's a dangerous type of sport and yet it's fun.)

In the night I sally forth to seek my quarry
And I find I forgot to bring my gun!

I am lost in the jungle
All alone and unarmed
When I meet a lioness in her lair!

Then I'm glad to be back in my own little corner,
All alone
      In my own
            Little chair.

(continued from page 3)

prin - cess or a milk - maid,_____ I'm the great - est pri - ma don - na in Mi -

lan._____ I'm an heir - ess who has al - ways had her

silk made _____ By her own flock of silk - worms in Ja -

pan._____ I'm a girl men go mad for, love's a